Dear _____,

Happy Valentine's
Day
(and happy every-
day, too!)

Love,

Granny + Pop
2/91

Crocus in the Snow

Crocus
in the
Snow

A
Book
of
Poems
by

Joan Walsh Anglund

Random House 🏠 New York

Library of Congress Cataloging-in-Publication Data

Anglund, Joan Walsh.

Crocus in the snow : a book of poems / by Joan Walsh Anglund.

p. cm.

ISBN 0-394-58436-8

I. Title.

PS3551.N47C7   1990   90-53125

811'.54—dc20

Manufactured in the United States of America

24689753

First Edition

FOR TRICIA,
...WITH LOVE

Love
is at the beginning

and ending
of
all
things.

I have not the beauty of perfection
      ...the strength of wisdom
           the wide view of knowledge
                 the clear eye of faith

     I have only
        the small whisper
             ...of Hope.

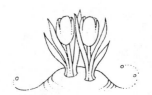

Like a crocus
            in the snow,
      ...I stand
            knee-deep in Winter,
      holding
            Springtime
                  in my heart!

Our days

       may be numbered

but our love

       can be limitless.

That which we think
creates
that which will be.

Under the snow of long Winter
lies
the seed of Spring.

As the seed beneath the snow
is
the soul of man,

...waiting
to awaken
to its fruitfulness
and
use.

The eyes of Love
see
only
Beauty!

With release

        comes Peace.

Let me learn

        to Love

                …without holding,

        to Give

                …without expecting

                        to receive in return.

Do not be dazzled
                    by flattering words,
        for they are
                    as the sunlight
                                upon the shallow waters,

        …lovely
                    for their instant,

                …but soon
                            gone!

The minutes chatter

...the centuries
                    are still.

Adversity
        often
        activates
   a strength
          we did not know
               we had!

Beauty
arranges itself

in the folds and crevices
of Nature,
…and
waits,

to be discovered!

In a precarious world,
we each
find our Safety,
...and name it
"Home"!

Our lives
            are as small
    as
        the fear
                we allow.

Sometimes,

       our greatest Strength

     is

       admitting our Weakness.

Not one

        among us

    is

        Perfect,

    ...and yet,

            we, each,

                are Loved!

Faith
    shall finish

all
  that
    Hope begins.

From the dust

        of our Yesterdays

We must shape

        our bright Tomorrows.

We cannot stop

the wind

from blowing,

…but,

we *can*

set our sails,

…so it helps us

on our way!

Until
you know
another's Pain,

You cannot know
his Reasons.

In War,

      ...or Peace,

   ...the wrens

         still

            build their nests.

Nothing
        stirs
     as easily
        as Fear,

   ...and Cruelty,
            his darker twin,
      awakens
            soon after!

Farewell,

     …my beloved Friend,

     …my companion,

         in many Dreams.

I release you,

     at last,

     …not in sadness,

         but,

           …in *Joy*!

For

   the song you brought

   shall "sing"

      forever

        …within my heart!

As the waves
            that rise and fall

        are the events
                of this world,

As the sure and steady tide
                    beneath,
        is the movement
                of the Spirit.

It is never too late

            nor too early

                       to Love,

     ...for the time

             to Love

               is

                    always "NOW"!

Let
    each Day
            find us
    making
        some advance
                against the Darkness.

59

A day shall come
        when we shall not
                    hold these hands,
            ...nor "see"
                    these dear "familiar" faces,
Therefore,
            let us cherish
                    our Loved ones
                    <u>NOW,</u>
        ...while there is time,
    and hold them close,
                ...and treat them
                            with all great tenderness

for, soon,
            ...so soon,
        we must part,
                ...and we shall not
                        "find" them again

            until we meet, once more,
                    in
                        Eternity!

Love
    shall lead us
where
    we need
        to go.

About the Author

JOAN WALSH ANGLUND, the much loved author/illustrator of such celebrated titles as *A Friend Is Someone Who Likes You* and *Love Is a Special Way of Feeling*, lives with her family in an eighteenth-century house in Connecticut.

Mrs. Anglund was honored by the Lincoln Academy of Illinois for her contribution to literature and art. Her books, which have sold more than thirty million copies, have been widely published all around the world in over fourteen languages.